IMAGES
of America

NACOGDOCHES

Located on the southeast corner of Plaza Principal, Nacogdoches's town square, this century-old building and the lot it occupies have witnessed virtually all of the town's history since European intervention. Located approximately 200 feet from the original site of the Old Stone Fort, the John S. Roberts home occupied the area until it burned around 1900. The present building was constructed in 1907, and its upper floors served as a mercantile store and the site of Stone's Café, where a young Bonnie Parker worked as a waitress. At various times, blacksmiths or barbers labored in its bottom story. Steve Hartz, seated with a banjo on the curb, acquired the building in 1978 as a home for his Old Time String Shop, which is heated in winter by a wood stove and cooled only by summer breezes. Hartz and friends gather there on Saturday afternoons for an old-fashioned jam of traditional music. (Photograph by Hardy Meredith.)

On the Cover: The Old Stone Fort, originally known as *casa de piedras*, was constructed by Antonio Gil Y'Barbo, founder of Nacogdoches, as a place to conduct his official business as chief of militia and civil affairs for this Spanish frontier outpost. The structure thus took on a public nature, although it remained privately owned until razed in 1902 to make way for modern business establishments, including Swift Brothers and Smith Drug Store. (Courtesy of the East Texas Research Center.)

Archie P. McDonald and Hardy Meredith

ISBN 978-1-5316-5188-6

Published by Arcadia Publishing
Charleston SC, Chicago IL, Portsmouth NH, San Francisco CA

Library of Congress Control Number: 2009928854

For all general information contact Arcadia Publishing at:
Telephone 843-853-2070
Fax 843-853-0044
E-mail sales@arcadiapublishing.com
For customer service and orders:
Toll-Free 1-888-313-2665

Visit us on the Internet at www.arcadiapublishing.com

To: Jeri, Hardy C., Heath Dale, Blake, Jaxon Hardy, and Carley Meredith, and to Judy, Kelly, Tucker, Christopher, and Janet McDonald

Contents

ACKNOWLEDGMENTS

Citizens of Nacogdoches often refer to their hometown as "The Oldest Town In Texas," a title appropriated for it by Lucille Fain, wife of *Daily Sentinel* publisher Victor B. Fain and a reporter and columnist for the paper for decades. However many partisans of other Texas cities may dispute Mrs. Fain's claim, the title has worked its way into the pine trees and creeks and red hills that have hosted a community of peoples—Caddo, Spanish, Mexican, Texian, and finally general Americans—who have occupied the area for centuries and are pretty much permanent now. Mrs. Fain did as much as anyone to preserve the multiple heritages of Nacogdoches, and it is fitting that she be remembered now.

R. B. Blake, a county clerk with enough time to translate Spain's archives concerning Nacogdoches into English, and George Louis Crocket, the first instructor of history at Stephen F. Austin State Teachers College, now University, took a turn at preserving Nacogdoches's history. Modern organizations such as Historic Nacogdoches, Inc., and the Nacogdoches County Historical Commission, along with the City of Nacogdoches through its Main Street, landmarks, historic districts, and maintenance of historic properties through statues, markers, and preservation efforts, all play rich roles in keeping modern-day people aware of the ways of their predecessors.

Many individuals have made and continue to make significant contributions in the historicity of Nacogdoches. They are legion, but F. E. Abernethy must be mentioned. "Ab" rebuilds trails where surely Caddo trod, constructs museum exhibits, makes speeches, and keeps us always aware of obligations that are ours because we occupy the narrow part of the hourglass of history.

We wish to acknowledge the considerable assistance of Linda Reynolds, director of the East Texas Research Center; Carolyn Spears of the Old Stone Fort Museum; Texas Historical Commission; SFA's Department of Social and Cultural Analysis; Mary Ann Young; Charlotte Stokes; P. R. Blackwell; Virginia Mize Abernathy; *Daily Sentinel*; Nacogdoches Memorial Hospital; Nacogdoches Medical Center; City of Nacogdoches Historic Properties; Chris Talbot; Norman Johnson; Dwayne Prestwood; and Hardy Meredith. Above all, thanks to Portia Gordon for her indispensible efforts assembling the illustrations and preparing the manuscript.

INTRODUCTION

Nacogdoches, located in the heart of the pine forests of East Texas, hosted Caddo villages long before Fr. Antonio Jesus de Margil arrived in 1716 to found one of six missions he established in East Texas. All six missions served God and the government of Spain as religious conversion centers and territorial signposts to the French—as close as Natchitoches, Louisiana—that this Texas part of the New World was off limits to their schemes of westward expansion.

The government of Spain got the most results from the joint venture, because France was gone from the continent by 1763, but so few Caddo had accepted Christianity that the absence of the French threat enabled Spain to close its East Texas missions and also require families that had established farms or ranches near them to withdraw to San Antonio in 1773. Antonio Gil Y'Barbo emerged as a leader of those refugees and led them back eastward to found the modern city of Nacogdoches in April 1779. The town's name was derived from the tribe of Caddo who lived along its Banita and La Nana Creeks.

Y'Barbo built his stone house, later known as the Old Stone Fort, on a corner of the Plaza Principal, the civic center of his community; a church square lay approximately 100 yards to the west. Y'Barbo made land grants, commanded the militia, and acted as liaison between the Spanish government and people of Nacogdoches until he was exiled because of forbidden trading activities.

Nacogdoches became the starting place of two schemes to seize part of Texas from Spain, the Gutierrez-Magee Expedition of 1812 and the James Long venture in 1819, both failures. When legal Anglo settlements began under Mexican authority in the 1820s, *empresario* Haden Edwards received the land around Nacogdoches to convey to settlers and then led the unsuccessful Fredonia Rebellion against Mexico. Nacogdoches was also the scene of one of the first disturbances of the Texas Revolution in 1832 and the destination of refugees during the Runaway Scrape in 1836.

Nacogdoches was the first home in Texas to Sam Houston, leader of the revolutionary army and first president of the Republic of Texas; he and Thomas J. Rusk, also of Nacogdoches, served as the first two United States senators from Texas. Others citizens prominent in the era included Adolphus Sterne, financier of the New Orleans Greys who fought at the battles at the Alamo and Goliad; and Charles S. Taylor, a signer of the Declaration of Independence of Texas.

In the first period of statehood, 1846–1860, the Nacogdoches population reflected its Southern heritage in its rural, agricultural orientation. Frederick Voigt led the first volunteers from Nacogdoches to the Civil War, and although no battles of that conflict occurred in the region, Nacogdoches joined the rest of the failed Confederacy in economic loss and significant social change.

The population began to grow again after the arrival of the Houston, East and West Texas Railroad in 1883, or HE&WT—"Hell Either Way Taken" according to some. The first banks appeared in the 1890s, but the first permanent ones, Commercial and Stone Fort, did not appear until 1901 and 1903, respectively.

The Stone Fort Rifles, another volunteer group, represented Nacogdoches in the Spanish-American War in 1898, as did doughboys in World War I, this time as individual enlistees or because they received greetings from Uncle Sam. Even more did so in World War II, Korea, Vietnam, Iraq, and scores of other 20th- and 21st-century deployments.

The founding of Stephen F. Austin State Teachers College in 1923, and Texas Farm Products in 1930, provided profound economic stimulus and social adjustment for Nacogdoches. The college, located approximately one mile north of the town square, ultimately employed nearly 1,000 professors, staff, and support personnel and attracted 12,000 potential scholars with considerable disposable income, which has resulted in many an apartment complex and pizza and burger provider. Texas Farm Products, a manufacturer of fertilizer and animal feeds and products, became the city's first real industry; sawmills, electrical transformer makers, RV manufacturers, canners, valve and seal makers, and dozens of other industries have joined them since 1930.

Nacogdoches markets its history in several preservation districts and features the Adolphus Sterne Home, the Old University Building, a replica of the Old Stone Fort located on the university campus, a restoration village known as Millard's Crossing, the Convention and Visitor's Bureau located on the square in a 1917 post office building, and the city-operated railroad depot and Taylor-Acosta House, likely the senior structure extant in town. The city celebrates its past in an annual Heritage Festival, the diversity of its more than 32,000 souls in a Multi-Cultural Festival, and its economy in a Blueberry Festival.

Nacogdoches proudly hosts Hotel Fredonia, perhaps the first community-owned hotel in the United States, though now privately operated and the administrator of its convention center. Its citizens also welcomed thousands of coastal refugees from Hurricanes Katrina, Rita, Gustav, and Ike and mourned with the rest of the world when the space shuttle *Columbia* descended upon them from the heavens.

The city's people may attend over 50 houses of worship representing almost as many denominations. They belong to organizations as varied as AA and archeologists, Freemasons and Knights of Columbus, garden clubs and health advocates, Rotary and Pilot, and photograph enthusiasts, who may enjoy or critique this publication!

Nacogdoches, then, is the sum of its history and its parts—part Spanish, Mexican, Anglo, African American, and Asian, and in the language of the census, other; part male and female; part old and part young; representing every part of the world, various political views, and differing economic pursuits; some drive Fords, some Toyotas, and a few Mercedes—all citizens of one community in East Texas as wide as the world and as old as time. This is part of our story in images and words.

One

The First Century —Or So

The Caddo were the earliest people to inhabit portions of Oklahoma, Arkansas, Louisiana, and eastern Texas, including Nacogdoches. The Caddo lived in villages usually stretched along streams of water such as Banita and La Nana bayous, or creeks, in conical structures. Because of abundant resources in the forests and streams where they lived, they were not overly aggressive but were willing to defend their homes. Many Caddo perished as a result of European diseases, and after the arrival of Anglos, only a remnant survived to move to Indian Territory or Oklahoma. (Painting by Nola Davis, courtesy of the Texas Historical Commission.)

This Caddo mound is located in the front yard at 516 Mound Street. Previous owners of the home behind it, Mr. and Mrs. Thomas Reavley, prevented archeological examination of the mound, fearing for the safety of the giant oak tree growing there, but subsequent owners Dr. Robert and Ruth Carroll did permit Stephen F. Austin State University professor Dr. James Corbin to conduct a dig there. Corbin's work revealed evidence that this was a Caddo burial mound. Below is a map of the mound site. (Photograph courtesy of Carolyn Spears and the Old Stone Fort Museum; map courtesy of the Department of Social and Cultural Analysis at Stephen F. Austin State University.)

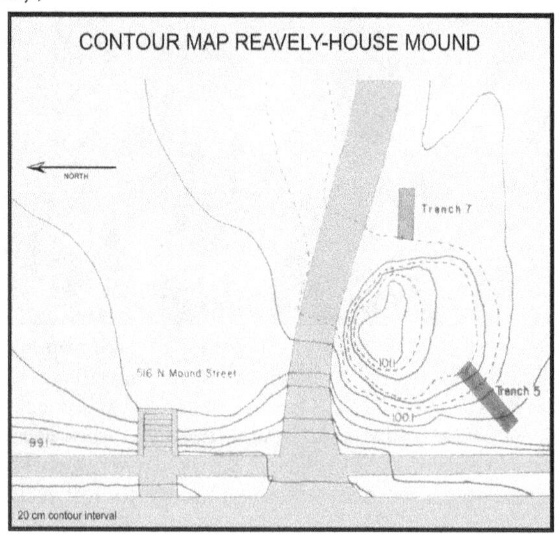

Pictured here is the Nacogdoches University Building as it appeared in 1890. The university received its charter in 1846, the last educational institution authorized by the Congress of the Republic of Texas. This structure was erected on Washington Square, just north of the town's square, in 1858. Nacogdoches University operated as a subscription school under numerous sponsors, including its own trustees, the Catholic Church, and Milam Lodge No. 2 of the Ancient Free and Accepted Masons (AF&AM), and for a time was rented to a college whose own building had burned. The building served as a hospital and barracks for Confederates during the Civil War and for Union soldiers after the conflict. It became the property of the Nacogdoches Independent School District (NISD) in 1904, and the Federation of Women's Clubs are responsible for its operation as a museum facility and for receptions. (Courtesy of the East Texas Research Center.)

Left is John Durst Sr., who came to Texas in 1812 as an Indian trader employed by Samuel Davenport, a partner in the trading business of Davenport and Barr, previously located east of the square downtown on what is now East Main Street. Davenport and Barr became Spanish subjects and received permission to open their trading post in Nacogdoches in the 1790s. Durst Street in Nacogdoches is named for Durst's family. Below are members of the Durst and Peyton Edwards Smith families at a tea party in 1866. From left to right are (seated) Nellie Edwards Sparks, Mrs. Edwards, Mrs. S. A. Durst, her mother Mrs. Hart, and Mrs. E. J. Fry, with Haden Edwards in front; (standing) Peyton Edwards Smith, unidentified, Dr. Smith, Mr. E. J. Fry, Bell Edwards, and Lena Durst. (Both courtesy of East Texas Research Center.)

Right, Charles Stanfield Taylor, a native of England, settled in Nacogdoches late in the 1820s. Taylor married Anna Marie Rouff, sister of Adolphus Sterne's wife, Eva Rosine Rouff, and so these pioneer citizens of Nacogdoches were brothers-in-law. Taylor served the community as a member of the *ayuntamiento*, or town council, fought in the Battle of Nacogdoches, and signed the Texas Declaration of Independence. He is buried in Oak Grove Cemetery. Below, Thomas Jefferson Rusk, a native of Georgia, arrived in Texas in 1835. He served as secretary of war in the interim revolutionary government of Texas, chaired the constitutional convention for the new state of Texas in 1845, and was one of Texas's first two U.S. senators. He is buried in Oak Grove Cemetery. (Both courtesy of the East Texas Research Center.)

Nicholas Adolphus Sterne left Cologne, Germany, immigrated to New Orleans in 1816, and became a peddler in the Mississippi Valley. He visited Nacogdoches in 1826 and then moved to the city two years later. Sterne's home on Lanana Street, where he entertained visitors such as Sam Houston and the Raguet family, became a frontier salon. He recruited and financed the New Orleans Greys, who fought in the Texas Revolution at the Alamo and at Goliad. Sterne served in many public offices in Nacogdoches, including postmaster and primary judge. He also served in the Congress of the Republic of Texas. Below is Anna Raguet, who captured the fancy of Sam Houston during his stay with the Sterne family. She was a daughter of Henry Raguet and later married Dr. Robert Irion, also a participant in the Texas Revolution. (Both courtesy of the East Texas Research Center.)

Confederate veterans assembled on the square in front of the Old Stone Fort. Recruits gathered there in the spring of 1861 and elected Frederick Voigt their commander. Most of the men from Nacogdoches remained west of the Mississippi River during the Civil War, fighting in battles such as one in Mansfield, Louisiana, in April 1864, which repulsed a Union effort to enter Texas via the Red River. Veterans rallied at the fort annually on Confederate Memorial Day as long as they were able to do so. Below is another view of Plaza Principal, or the town square, with the Old Stone Fort in the center at the end of the block. Stone Fort Bank, now Regions Bank, later occupied the corner site advertising 5¢ cigars. Transportation in 1899 still depended on real horsepower, but the utility pole indicates that electric service, established in the 1880s, was available. (Both courtesy of the East Texas Research Center.)

This historic elm tree, located on the bank of Banita Creek not far from Plaza Principal, provided shade for many gatherings such as political rallies and picnics in Nacogdoches during the 19th century. This photograph from 1890 shows the sparse development of the area. Below is the Banita Hotel, located on Pilar Street. The Banita was one of many hotels and boardinghouses located near the tracks of the Houston, East and West Texas Railroad for the convenience of travelers. The iron bridge spans Banita Creek, one of two creeks that attracted the Caddo and then Spanish missionaries to the area centuries earlier. (Both courtesy of the East Texas Research Center.)

The Old Stone Fort was built by Antonio Gil Y'Barbo, founder of Nacogdoches, as his headquarters. Because of Y'Barbo's official role as captain of military and political representative of the Spanish government, the Old Stone Fort, or house, assumed a public nature it never lost despite remaining private property until razed in 1902. By the time this picture was taken, the old building had fallen from favor and was host to a saloon. The second story access off the balcony on the east face had been altered with the elimination of steps and the addition of a lean-to shed. Below, the Reverend George Louis Crocket painted this scene of the south side of Plaza Principal in 1903. The central building was the courthouse of Nacogdoches County, one of five structures that have served as the seat on county government in Nacogdoches. This painting was taken from a postcard. (Both courtesy of the East Texas Research Center.)

Above is a western view of Plaza Principal, still an open plaza and the last remaining architectural evidence of the founding of Nacogdoches by Spanish officials. Residents and visitors to the downtown area congregated here to conduct business and exchange views. The covered facility in the center was the site of the town well. Below, old-time fiddlers, identified as Boss Fiddlers, a musical group from Nacogdoches in the last quarter of the 19th century, posed for this photograph. Typical of the custom of the time, the senior fiddlers, seated, are bearded, but the younger musicians standing have retreated to a mustache only. Fiddlers were in great demand throughout the nation to provide music for public dances. (Both courtesy of the East Texas Research Center.)

Lynn Taliaferro Barret, a native of Virginia, began exploring for oil in Nacogdoches County late in the 1850s. Edwin Drake drilled the first oil well in America near Titusville, Pennsylvania, in 1859, and Barret's discovery of oil in a shallow pool in the southern part of Nacogdoches County in September 1866 led to the first oil well in Texas and the first west of the Mississippi River. Since 1866, the area has been known as Oil Springs. Barret's discovery was a harbinger for Texas more than for Nacogdoches, because oil in that area of Texas was shallow and limited. In the future, however, the area was discovered to contain significant stores of oil and natural gas. Above, the first wooden storage tanks in Texas stored oil from the field Barret discovered. Later he delivered the oil via the first pipeline in Texas. Below, unidentified drillers labor to complete a well in the Oil Springs area. (Both courtesy of the East Texas Research Center.)

The Benevolent and Protective Order of Elks lodge in Nacogdoches supported a marching band, led by Tony Cruz from Cuba, that provided music for parades and concerts in the downtown area. This picture features the band in the 300 block of East Main Street near the later site of Cason, Monk, and Company on the north and Schmidt's on the right. Below are members of the band, from left to right, (first row) Ashel Mintz, Conrad Rusche, Cecil Hardeman, George Ingraham, Charles Shindler, Riley Henson, Dan Jinkins, Maury Haltom, and O. E. Hubbard; (second row) Louis Mueller, Clyde Stegal, Herbert Schmidt, John Thomas, Dumas Simpson, Ray Buchanan, Tony Cruz, Vinson Davidson, and Ernest Spradley; (third row) W. P. Ingraham, unidentified, mascot Lorena Middlebrook, Thomas E. Baker, Fritz Swift, Will Pressler, and M. Stroud. (Both courtesy of the East Texas Research Center.)

The Southern cotton culture arrived in East Texas before the Civil War and lingered until the mid-20th century. Slaves produced the cotton on some pre–Civil War farms, but white farmers produced the majority of the product with their own labor. After the Civil War, the sharecrop system was practiced in Nacogdoches County, as well as the rest of the South. The area hosted a score or more of gins early in the 1900s, but none operated there by the 1960s. Above, a late 19th-century farmer brings his bales down East Main Street, bound for the railroad depot located west of the downtown area. Below, another farmer also brought his cotton bales to market. Both used oxen rather than mules as draft animals. (Both courtesy of the East Texas Research Center.)

Several newspapers have been published in Nacogdoches since late in the 19th century, including the *Chronicle*, a predecessor of the *Daily Sentinel*, founded by Giles Haltom, which has been in business for over a century. Above, publisher Will Haltom stands in the doorway of the Chronicle Building with his daughter, Ruby, in 1897. Below, in a photograph taken a few years later, Haltom may be seen in the open door of the renamed and relocated *Daily Sentinel*, behind Ruby and Maury (on horse) Haltom, on horseback. The brick construction of both buildings was a typical construction method for downtown structures. (Both courtesy of the East Texas Research Center.)

Commercial National Bank, founded in 1901, was located in this building on the northeast corner of East Main and Church Streets. Commercial National Bank moved westward to an interior location in the 200 block of East Main, near Stripling's Drug Store, and by 2000 had expanded to nearly an entire block bordered by East Main, South Fredonia, Hospital, and South Pecan Streets. In the photograph above, several citizens pass the day leaning on the building's support structure. Below is the interior of J. R. Isaac's Store, a shopping emporium located in downtown Nacogdoches at the end of the 19th century. Four storekeepers were available to assist this lone, diminutive shopper. (Both courtesy of the East Texas Research Center.)

Above are members of Nacogdoches's senior literary and social organization for women, the Cum Concilio Club, which saved the stones of the Old Stone Fort in 1902 and stored them on Washington Square for future use. Members are, from left to right, (first row) Mesdames C. D. Stinson, E. C. Branch, C. H. Butt, Roland Jones, John Garrison, and Lloyd Bowers; (second) Mesdames George Davidson, George Matthews, R. C. Shindler, Pratt Matthews, and E. M. Dotson; (third row) Mesdames ? Ratcliff, W. F. Price, S. W. Blount, F. C. Ford, Robert Lindsay, and Jule Smith. Below are the contemporary members of the Cum Concilio Club, (seated) Mesdames Tom Wright, David Shofner, Ray Rinker, Jack Mathews, George Millard, Robert Lawson, and Ron Collins; (standing) Mesdames M. S. Wright III, John Ruckel, Carl Smith, Arthur Speck, Jerry Sutton, and Chris Kline. Members not shown include Mesdames Frazier Arwood, O'Neal Dubberly, Rick Hurst, Jim Kingham, John Mast, Robert Palm, and Ms. Nancy Tipton. (Above courtesy East Texas Research Center; below courtesy Hardy Meredith.)

As did many cities located in western America late in the 19th century, Nacogdoches citizens maintained vigilance through a local militia known as the Stone Fort Rifles. Above, members of the militia company muster before their tents for the inspection of their elected officers and their mascot, or sweetheart, Hittie Clark. The Stone Fort Rifles became Company B, 2nd Texas Regiment, in 1898 when the United States and Spain engaged in that "splendid little war" that lasted only four months and made the United States an international force. Below, the company, still calling itself the Stone Fort Rifles, boarded the railcar that took them away to war. The company returned to Nacogdoches before the year ended. (Both photographs by Schlueter's Studio in Nacogdoches, courtesy of the East Texas Research Center.)

Formal education developed slowly in Nacogdoches without a public school system until the 20th century. Previously, students could attend a variety of subscription schools, such as those operated before the Civil War by Prof. Marcus Montross; attend Nacogdoches University under various administrations, including Milam Lodge No. 2, AF&AM, and the Roman Catholic Church; or perhaps Jennie Harris's school, located on Walker Avenue. Jennie Harris is shown above in 1895 with her students, who ranged in grade level from primaries to the fifth or sixth grade. Below, an unidentified but daring young lady climbed aboard the cab of Engine No. 25, one of the locomotives operated by Frost Lumber Company to move its logs and lumber. The engine, built in 1894, was previously used by the New York Elevated Train System. (Both courtesy of the East Texas Research Center.)

Above is the interior of the post office in Nacogdoches with postmaster H. H. Cooper at work. This remained the city's post office until a new facility was constructed in the center of Plaza Principal in 1918. Below, Christ Church, the historic Episcopal church in Nacogdoches, was built in 1890 and located on what was called Church Street because of its presence. The congregation worshiped in this facility before moving to a brick edifice on the southeast corner of Mound Street and Starr Avenue, where it also operates a school for the elementary grades. The Reverend George Louis Crocket, a pastor of Christ Church, carved portions of its altar. (Both courtesy of the East Texas Research Center.)

Enduring symbols of Nacogdoches include the Old Stone Fort, seen above, and Banita and La Nana Creeks, two streams that drain Nacogdoches on their way to joining south of the downtown area before continuing southward toward the Angelina River. Antonio Gil Y'Barbo constructed what he identified as a *casa de piedras*, or stone house, but others called it a stone fort because of its solid construction. Likely it was the only two-story structure in East Texas constructed by Europeans for some time. Workmen razed his building in 1902, but others built a replica of it on the campus of Stephen F. Austin State College in 1936. The replica is remarkably similar except that the stairs are reversed. The creeks first provided water for a cluster of Caddo, then in turn for generations of Spanish, Mexican, and Anglo settlers, as seen below, when a group of Nacogdoches citizens went fishing around 1900. (Both courtesy of the East Texas Research Center.)

Two

The Way We Were

Above, East Texas doughboys don their World War I uniforms. These members of the Sergeants Battery, Company F, 64th Artillery, included several men from Nacogdoches. They are identified simply as, from left to right, (kneeling) Weeks, Smith, Fauset, and Meador; (standing) Mast, Mettauer, Muller, Cordell, Erwln, Reese, Adair, Mentzel, Rhodes, Perkins, Herbold, Davidson, and Hess. (Courtesy of the East Texas Research Center.)

Nacogdoches's central downtown square remained an open plaza from 1779, when Antonio Gil Y'Barbo founded the community, until 1917, when the Wilson administration erected a new post office building there. Over the years a covered town well, hitching rails, and other intrusions appeared, but essentially the area's open, public nature reflected the city's Spanish origins. That ended when construction began on the post office building. The photograph above shows the foundation and basement area of the building and the upper floors of downtown businesses located on the square's north side. Below, a photograph taken in August 1917 features the upper floor of the post office with construction scaffolding still in place. (Both courtesy of the East Texas Research Center.)

Nacogdoches began to change in some ways, but in other ways remained the same. The photograph above shows East Main Street looking eastward after the completion of the post office in the center of the square in 1917. Stone Fort Bank, which began in 1903 in a structure situated at the approximate vantage point of the camera, had moved across the square to the corner of Fredonia and East Main Streets. Swift Brothers and Smith Drug Store occupied the opposing corner, and the City Café operated near the other end of the block on the north side of the square. Below is the family of Amos Henderson Sr., on the right with Bible in hand, proclaiming the Word to his family. From left to right are wife Eula Mae, Charles Dale, Amos Jr., Helen Augusta, Harold Lloyd, Beau Lillie, and Earline. Henderson was a bi-vocational minister, otherwise working on a farm operated by McNeil Grimes. (Both courtesy of the East Texas Research Center.)

The Old Stone Fort had been among the first buildings constructed by Spaniards when they arrived to found Nacogdoches. It remained on the northeast corner of the town square until 1902, when W. U. Perkins purchased and destroyed the building to make way for a modern business establishment over the opposition of the members of Cum Concilio Club, a ladies' literary society. The club saved some of the stones and in 1907 erected a one-story structure with them on Washington Square. In 1936, the New Deal constructed a replica of the building on the campus of Stephen F. Austin State College. The photograph above was taken during dedication ceremonies on October 16, 1936. Below is Dr. Alton W. Birdwell, first president of Stephen F. Austin State College, who served the college from 1923 until his retirement in 1942. (Both courtesy of the East Texas Research Center.)

This photograph of Stone Fort National Bank appeared on a postcard during the 1940s. Stone Fort National Bank occupied the opposite corner of Fredonia and East Main Streets from its namesake building constructed by Antonio Gil Y'Barbo. The bank began operations on the west side of the square, moved to the north side after a few years, and finally located permanently on the east side. The large corner window was converted into a door for a while, but after a remodeling in the 1970s, the entrance was moved back to Main Street. The corner was then faced with stones that approximated the appearance of the original Stone Fort. The bank is a branch of Regions Bank. (Both courtesy of the East Texas Research Center.)

Dr. Paul L. Boynton, a native of central Texas who had trained at Peabody College in Nashville, Tennessee, a headquarters for educational training in the South, succeeded Dr. A. W. Birdwell as president of Stephen F. Austin State College in 1942. Juanita Boynton poses here with Dr. Boynton in their official residence located on the college campus. Dr. Boynton soon became a respected member of the Nacogdoches community. (Courtesy of the East Texas Research Center.)

Nacogdoches hosted the government of the Department of Nacogdoches under the government of Mexico and became a county as soon as Texas became a state. Following the Spanish model, its courthouses—there have been five—were never located in the center of the town square, although three courthouses were located on the side of the square. The courthouse shown above, the fourth in the county's history, was located on the southwest corner of the intersection of East Main and North South Streets from the early years of the 20th century until demolished in the 1950s to make way for its replacement on the same site. Below, a committee plans for a community homecoming in May 1936 in observance of the Texas Centennial. Seated are, from left to right, A. J. Thompson, Virginia Sanders, Mrs. Eugene Blount, Mrs. Elbert Reese, and H. B. Tucker; standing are Joe Mock (left) and B. H. Mize. (Courtesy of the East Texas Research Center.)

Among the social organizations on the campus of Stephen F. Austin State College when Dr. Paul L. Boynton became president was the Grand Order of Royal Barristers, a pre-law club. The club's members in 1942 included from left to right, (first row) Dan Mize, Billie Jones, John Bain, Bob Murphey, W. H. Jones, and Mathie Dearmond; (second row) sponsor Dr. W. R. Davis, Jodie Johnson, G. W. Martin, Don McLaughlin, Selwin Jones, and Dean James Allen; (third row) Harold Ross, James Hughes, Harlan McBee, Loran Perritte, Leslie Shellburne, John Shaddix, and unidentified; (fourth row) Winton and Quinton Lawrence, John Honea, Claude Banks, and Pat Gatewood. Below, with so many of the college's male students in the military services, Dr. Boynton rented some of the campus for training members of the Women's Auxiliary Army Corps, later known as WACs. Here several of the trainees have their shoes shined for inspection. (Above courtesy of the East Texas Research Center; below courtesy of Marguerite Crouse Bezanson.)

The WACs who trained at Stephen F. Austin State College served their country during World War II and also helped save the college, whose enrollment had dropped to approximately 300 mostly female students because nearly all of the males had either enlisted or been drafted into military service. The WACs trained for office administrative duties on the college's idle typewriters and business machines and then took the place of soldiers in mostly stateside posts, releasing the men for more hazardous duty. No one asked the men how they felt about this. Here a WAC walks among the pine trees on the college campus after a rare ice storm in Nacogdoches. (Courtesy of the East Texas Research Center and Marguerite Crouse Bezanson.)

Mize Brothers Manufacturing Company, founded in the 1920s and in operation until the 1980s on North Street just a few blocks from the courthouse, produced dresses and other garments for women. The brothers were Byron and W. A. (better known as Mr. Allen) Mize, who owned businesses in Crockett, Texas, and Logansport, Louisiana, before coming to Nacogdoches to operate the dress factory and also a department store. The factory mostly employed women to produce the garments. The large, white brick building featured the layout center, shown above, and the assembly area, shown below, where women sewed the dresses together in row after row. The women held annual reunions for years after the factory closed. (Both courtesy of Virginia Mize Abernathy.)

"Main Street" in Nacogdoches is really East Main Street, and the square is the heart of the downtown business district and was home to the city's banks and most of its retail businesses until the 1960s. Above is a photograph of East Main Street on the north side of the square taken late in the 1940s. The corner of the county's fourth courthouse with its visible dome is at left center one block away from the square. Commercial National Bank still occupied its second home in the middle of the block, and E. C. Best Department Store was located next door. Below, a band marches in the homecoming parade on East Main Street. (Both courtesy of the East Texas Research Center.)

Dr. Ralph Wright Steen is shown with Gladys Steen in their official residence on the campus of Stephen F. Austin State College. Dr. Steen served as president of the college, which became a full-service university in 1968, from 1957 until his retirement in 1976. When he became president, enrollment had just exceeded 2,000 students, and it approached 13,000 students when he retired. Dr. Steen introduced the university's modern administrative structure. He also became a beloved leader of the community. The university's library was named in Dr. Steen's honor when he retired. (Courtesy of the East Texas Research Center.)

Main Street was busy on Saturday, July 16, 1968, for the annual Side Walk Sale sponsored by the Downtown Merchant's Association. Below, Charlotte Baker Montgomery, the daughter of Nacogdoches poet and novelist Karle Wilson Baker, became the city's leading literary figure in her own right in the field of children's literature. A Newberry Award winner, her stories featured animals, especially dogs, and young women. She donated property for and became a cofounder of the Nacogdoches Animal Shelter. (Both courtesy of the East Texas Research Center.)

As late as the 1960s, Nacogdoches was served by five drugstores, four of them located in the downtown area and one adjacent to City Memorial Hospital on Mound Street. Above is Stripling's Drug Store, founded in 1901 and operated by the Stripling family for most of the century. Stripling's Drug Store was located in the center of the block on the north side of the square. Turner's Drug Store, operated by Dick Turner, occupied the corner of East Main and North Church Street, on the second block east of the square. Below, Pam Perkins prepares to make a delivery in the store's Volkswagen with the mounted sign that proclaimed, "Have Pill Will Travel." (Above courtesy of Mary Ann Young; below courtesy the East Texas Research Center.)

Lenville Martin served as superintendent of Nacogdoches Independent School District (NISD) during the turbulence of racial integration in the 1960s and 1970s. Martin served the district as a classroom teacher, school principal, and superintendent in a career that extended over four decades. Martin is making a presentation at Hotel Fredonia while Dr. Tommy Franks, a member of the school board and chairman of the Department of Elementary Education at Stephen F. Austin State University, looks on. (Courtesy of the East Texas Research Center.)

Kathy Baker, Miss Nacogdoches in 1968 and a popular singer with the Tom Houston Orchestra and other musical groups in the East Texas area, sings for her supper in a meeting room at Hotel Fredonia. Later Mrs. Byron McGough, Kathy worked in the office of Dr. Robert Lehmann and continued to sing for groups and gatherings in the area. She and her brother, the late Tommy Baker, established a scholarship in the school of nursing at Stephen F. Austin State University in honor of their mother. (Courtesy of the East Texas Research Center.)

A. L. Mangham Jr., a graduate of Nacogdoches High School, joined the U.S. Navy the year before Japanese naval and air forces attacked U.S. military installations in Hawaii and elsewhere in the Pacific theater. Though always in the navy, Mangham served as a corpsman with the U.S. Marine Corps during World War II until wounded in the battle for Saipan. He remained in the navy after the war, received a commission, and served as a hospital administrator before retiring and returning to Nacogdoches for a second career as president of Fredonia State Bank and mayor of Nacogdoches. Above, Mangham chats with M. A. "Buddy" Anderson, owner of Anderson Grain Company, and below, he visits with Robert Monk of Cason, Monk Hardware. (Both courtesy of the East Texas Research Center.)

Community and civic leaders and all Fredonia State Bank investors and officers, seen above, are, from left to right, M. M. Stripling, also a former mayor of Nacogdoches; J. Elbert Reese, owner of several businesses in Nacogdoches including an automobile agency; and Roland Vannoy, chairman of the bank's board of directors. Bank president A. L. Mangham Jr., who also served as mayor of Nacogdoches, is seated. Below, Nacogdoches contractor and former mayor Bob Muckleroy accepts a check from Tommy Williams, president of Stone Fort National Bank. (Both courtesy of the East Texas Research Center.)

Tom and Peggy Wright are shown above with their daughter Peggy. Both Mr. and Mrs. Wright were active in business and community affairs. Tom Wright was a salesman, president, and eventually chairman of the board of directors of Texas Farm Products, a company founded by M. S. Wright in Nacogdoches in 1930. Mrs. Wright served three terms on the board of regents for Stephen F. Austin State University and is a member of the board of directors of Citizens Bank. The music building on the university campus is named for Tom and Peggy Wright. Below, Nacogdoches High School Dragon fans Dr. James G. Taylor, James Milstead, and Superintendent Lenville Martin gather on the drill field to watch their favorite team practice. (Both courtesy of the East Texas Research Center.)

Bob Murphey, a professional master of ceremonies and humorist, established a national speaking business from a base in Nacogdoches. Murphey lost an arm in an accident, while still a teenager. Still, he served in the merchant marines during World War II and as a volunteer fireman in Nacogdoches for half a century. Murphey served as district attorney before show business gradually became his career. Murphey appeared on stages in virtually every state in the nation and on the television show *Hee Haw* with his clean, rural humor. (Courtesy of the East Texas Research Center.)

Above, Dr. Ralph W. Steen, president of Stephen F. Austin State University, presents the university's Distinguished Professor Award to Dr. F. E. Abernethy, professor of English and director of the Texas Folklore Society. Below, a group of community leaders gather in the University Center. From left to right are (first row) university president Ralph W. Steen, vice president for academic affairs John T. Lewis III, county judge Carl Burrows, district judge Jack Pierce, and Sheriff John Lightfoot; (second row) attorney Billy Early, Nacogdoches city manager J. T. Alders, Mayor Bob Muckleroy, and police chief M. C. Roebuck. (Both courtesy of the East Texas Research Center.)

M. Steele Wright, president of Texas Farm Products, introduces Texas governor Dolph Briscoe when he stopped by to visit supporters at Hotel Fredonia. Wright came to Nacogdoches in 1930 when he was 16 years old and helped his father found Texas Farm Products. He later succeeded his father as president and chief operating officer of the firm. Below, Nacogdoches mayor Bob Muckleroy signs a purchase order while Nacogdoches police chief M. C. Roebuck, Smith-Mann Motor Company service manager Billy Warren, and Sheriff John Lightfoot look on. (Both courtesy of the East Texas Research Center.)

A phenomenon known as streaking, or running through a building or along a street unclothed, swept across the nation in March 1974. Nacogdoches and Stephen F. Austin State University did not escape the trend. A streaker shocked and amused the crowd in the campus dining room, among other areas, and reports of the incidents appeared in the *New York Times*. Pres. Ralph W. Steen, although embarrassed by the development, decided to close a street on campus between dormitories and allow streakers to proceed unclothed and unbothered by campus security to their hearts' content and to the amusement of the crowd who gathered to see the show, so long as they did not repeat the performance later. Steen's strategy worked, and the streaking stopped. (Courtesy of the East Texas Research Center.)

City Memorial Hospital was founded in the 1920s and continues into the 21st century as Nacogdoches Memorial Hospital. The City of Nacogdoches provided financial support for the hospital for a time, but then its elected trustees convinced voters to approve a 1¢ sales tax for its support. An elected board of trustees governs Nacogdoches Memorial Hospital. The original building, seen above, is no longer visible because of numerous additions and remodeling necessary to accommodate growth and keep pace with new developments. Below, one of those projects may be viewed in progress. Even this facade was altered dramatically in a renovation completed early in the 21st century. (Both courtesy of Nacogdoches Memorial Hospital.)

Oak Grove Cemetery, owned and maintained by the City of Nacogdoches, is not the oldest cemetery in Nacogdoches County but it does contain the remains of some of Nacogdoches's most notable citizens. Oak Grove Cemetery is the resting place of four signers of the Texas Declaration of Independence—Thomas J. Rusk, Charles Stanfield Taylor, William Clark, and John Forbes—and Texas Revolution figures Adolphus Sterne and Frost Thorne, plus Capt. Hayden Arnold, who led volunteers from Nacogdoches at the Battle of San Jacinto. It amuses residents that Hospital Street dead ends, so to speak, at the gate of their city's most famous cemetery. (Photograph by Hardy Meredith.)

Above, among the city's historic landmarks is the home of Adolphus Sterne, constructed on Lanana Street when he married Eva Rosine Rouff. The Sternes raised a large family in three spacious rooms with a sleeping loft and a wine cellar (something unusual for the Texas frontier). Sterne died in 1852, but Mrs. Sterne continued to live there until the property passed to the Von der Hoya family, who lived across Lanana Street. The Von der Hoya family conveyed the house to the City of Nacogdoches, as seen above, for use as a public library. The library moved elsewhere in the 1970s, but the Sterne-Hoya House, remains open to the public as a museum. (Both courtesy of the City of Nacogdoches, Department of Historic Properties.)

Located on North Street is what was once known as the Durst-Taylor House, and since its restoration as the Acosta-Taylor House, is one of the oldest structures in Nacogdoches, dating from the colonial period. The building was rescued by the McKinney Foundation and conveyed to the City of Nacogdoches. The photograph above shows both deterioration and modification from the building's original appearance, and the picture below shows the restoration supervised by Brian Bray, custodian of the city's historic properties. Bluebonnets bloom in the front yard, a historic garden grows on the south side of the building, and offices and an interpretative center are located behind the house. (Both courtesy of the City of Nacogdoches, Department of Historic Properties.)

The Houston, East and West Texas Railroad, built by Paul Bremond, reached Nacogdoches in 1883 and eventually connected the city to Houston and Shreveport, providing a market for the area's agricultural products and bringing the wider world to its doorstep. Other smaller lines—most associated with timber companies—developed, and the Cotton Belt, Southern Pacific, and eventually Union Pacific lines followed the HE&WT's path. Above is the railroad depot constructed in 1911 and used for passengers until that service ended in the 1950s. It was used as a company office even longer. Below is the depot restored to its original appearance under the supervision of Brian Bray, custodian of the city's historic properties. (Above photograph courtesy of City of Nacogdoches, Department of Historic Properties; below photograph by Clay Bostain, Creative Photography.)

Nacogdoches's art community received a boost in the 1970s when artists Reese and Lucille Kennedy opened Gallery 107 on the corner of Church and Pilar Streets. Above, Lucille Kennedy shows her watercolor, titled *Old Fashioned Roses*, in the gallery. At right, John Young stands beside the front door of Stripling's Drug Store in much the same way his grandfather had done when the drugstore opened. Young was the last member of the Stripling family associated with the store, which is still in business in a location on Mound Street under new management. Young operated Stripling's at its East Main Street location until it was destroyed by a fire that ravaged the north side of the town square in April 1984. He reopened in a new location on University Drive. (Above courtesy of the East Texas Research Center; below courtesy Mary Ann Young.)

Dr. James E. Corbin established classes in archaeology at Stephen F. Austin State University in the 1970s. Corbin introduced a series of summer digs to discover the archeological record of East Texas. He is shown here at work on Washington Square at a Caddo mound site in the summer of 1979. Corbin conducted similar investigations at the mound across Mound Street at the Reavley-Carroll House, the Adolphus Sterne House, the Blount House, and other sites in Nacogdoches and throughout Texas. Corbin also served as director of the Old Stone Fort Museum, located on the university campus. (Courtesy of Carolyn Spears and the Old Stone Fort Museum.)

Three

The Way We Are

Steve McCarty returned to Nacogdoches in August 1981 to take over as athletic director and head football coach of the Dragons at Nacogdoches High School (NHS). McCarty was as much cheerleader/motivator as coach, but by combining both skills, he led the Dragons far into the state playoffs within a few years. McCarty left NHS to become assistant athletic director at Stephen F. Austin State University and became director of athletics when his predecessor, Jim Hess, moved to New Mexico State University. McCarty retired in 2006 and was appointed to the university's board of regents in 2009. (Photograph by Hardy Meredith.)

Gov. Bill Clements came to Nacogdoches to participate in the dedication of a Texas Historical Commission historical marker on the home of Lynn Taliaferro Barret, who drilled the first oil well in Texas in Nacogdoches County in 1866. From left to right are Dr. Jere Jackson, chairman of the Nacogdoches County Historical Commission; Captain and Mrs. Charles Phillips, owners and restorers of the Barret House; Governor Clements; and state senator Roy Blake. Below is Nacogdoches Fire Department dispatcher Bill Day at his duty station. Day worked 24-hour shifts, so he had a cot nearby. (Both photographs by Hardy Meredith.)

Dr. William R. Johnson, above right, became the fourth president of Stephen F. Austin State University in 1976 following the retirement of Dr. Ralph W. Steen. Dr. Johnson, originally from Houston, previously served as vice president for academic affairs at Texas Tech University. He served as president of the university until his own retirement early in the 1990s. With him is Dr. Nancy Speck, vice president for development at the university. Below is Eddie Orum, Nacogdoches County agricultural extension agent and community leader. (Both photographs by Hardy Meredith.)

Campbell Cox went to work in the automotive tire agency and service station that his father, Navarro Cox, operated on the corner of North and East Main Streets across from the county courthouse, and when Campbell took over the business, he saw no reason to change its name. It remained the Navarro Cox Tire Company even after Cox moved the business to a new location on University Drive. When not marketing tires, Cox also operated a cattle ranch on land just east of the city of Nacogdoches and conducted other family-owned businesses and investments. (Photograph by Hardy Meredith.)

The smooth voice of Bill "Old Dad" Schultz emerged from many radios in Nacogdoches in the 1970s over KJCS Radio, broadcasting at 103.3 FM, when its format still included late night easy listening segments. Schultz also frequently served as master of ceremonies at community events. Below, another familiar radio voice, Bob Dunn, was co-owner of radio station KSFA. Dunn served as a pilot during the Korean Conflict, and he held a rank of colonel in the Confederate Air Force, an organization of preservers of vintage aircraft. Dunn provided play-by-play coverage for Nacogdoches Dragons and SFA Lumberjack football games. With Dunn at an air show in Nacogdoches in 1982 is Jeff Fain. (Both photographs by Hardy Meredith.)

This blended photograph of Nacogdoches's downtown square, or Plaza Principal, was produced by the class of Christopher Talbot, professor of photography at Stephen F. Austin State University, in the summer of 2008. The photograph was taken from precisely the same point atop a building that housed the Wilson Grain Company in 1882 and Region's Bank in 2008. The viewpoint looks west toward Banita Creek and the Union Pacific Railroad tracks. The left and upper portions depict the viewpoint from 1882 and the lower and right portions the modern era. Intrigued by the

town's past, art students at Stephen F. Austin State University, under the direction of assistant professor Christopher Talbot, set out to recapture historic locations throughout the town. Using old photographs found at the East Texas Research Center in SFA's Steen Library as a guide, the artists attempted to pinpoint the exact positions where the pictures were originally taken and re-photographed the area to show the development of Nacogdoches over the past 100 years. (Photograph courtesy of Christopher Talbot.)

Victor B. Fain, left (seated), went to work at the *Daily Sentinel* before World War II, served in the U.S. Navy during the war, and returned to the newspaper in 1946. Fain soon became editor and then publisher and continued in that capacity until local owners sold the paper to the Cox chain in the late 1980s. Fain proudly practiced booster journalism, claiming to favor anything good for Nacogdoches, and frequently ran this filler: "There are no strangers in Nacogdoches, only friends who have not met." He remained a beloved figure in the community until his death. With Fain is his son Ferris, who served as business manager of the newspaper. Below is the contemporary home of the *Daily Sentinel*, located at 4920 Colonial Drive. (Both photographs by Hardy Meredith.)

"Sugar and spice and everything nice. . . snaps and snails and puppy dog tails," argued an old explanation of little girls and boys, but another, better version claims that "all are precious in His sight." These photographs from the 1980s could be argued both ways! Right, five-year olds Karen Wunneburger, daughter of Mr. and Mrs. Richard Wunneburger, and Alexis Hutchison, daughter of Mr. and Mrs. Steve Hutchison, hunt Easter eggs hand in hand; below, seven-year olds Megan Goggins, daughter of Mr. and Mrs. Mike Goggins, cools down Ben Kennedy, son of Mr. and Mrs. Richard Kennedy, near his home on Walker Avenue. (Both photographs by Hardy Meredith.)

Dr. Francis Schott, left, with a friend, practiced medicine in a yellow frame house on Old Tyler Road beside the railroad tracks for generations and often dispensed wisdom along with injections and pills. Below are, from left to right, Debbie Tompkins, Mike Stowers, Keith Debury, John Dickey, and Drew Everett, members of Melrose, a band popular in Nacogdoches and in East Texas from 1979 through the mid-1980s. Tompkins was the featured vocalist with the group. This picture was taken in Snoopy's, a nightclub popular with university students. (Both photographs by Hardy Meredith.)

Bill Shaw, above, is a bullfighter—though sometimes billed as a rodeo clown—based in Nacogdoches. Shaw worked local high school and college rodeos before joining the professional rodeo circuit and frequently appeared in the Jaycee's Championship Rodeo held in the Nacogdoches Exposition Center. He also appeared in the National Rodeo Finals in 1981 and became active in the Christian rodeo ministry. At right, Wilford Jones is better known to Dallas Cowboys fans worldwide as Crazy Ray. Jones, who played defensive end on E. J. Campbell Black Dragon football teams coached by Bo McMichael in the 1950s, appointed himself the mascot of the Cowboys in 1962. He began by selling team pennants and eventually earned more television time than many Cowboys. Jones, shown here leading a parade in his hometown, died on March 17, 2007. (Both photographs by Hardy Meredith.)

A real Cowboy, quarterback "Dandy" Don Meredith, above, came to Nacogdoches in April 1984 to present the principal address to Lumberjack players and fans at Stephen F. Austin State University's annual sports banquet. At left, Myra Allen, the first queen of Nacogdoches's annual Heritage Festival, accepts her bouquet from festival chairman Tom Choate, president of the Nacogdoches County Chamber of Commerce and of Commercial Bank. Queen Myra was the daughter of Mr. and Mrs. Chester Allen. The Heritage Festival began in June 1984. (Both photographs by Hardy Meredith.)

"Burn, Baby, Burn!" may have echoed in the concrete canyons of Los Angeles and New York in the 1980s, but not in Nacogdoches, when the city suffered two catastrophic fires within 48 hours over a weekend in April 1984. Above, a fire started by arsonists in the Colony Mall, a shopping arcade located on the north side of the square, destroyed or damaged every building or business on the block and threatened the remainder of downtown. Below, on the following Monday afternoon, a welder's torch accidently sparked a fire that destroyed a wooden plywood manufacturing plant operated by International Paper. Property owners rebuilt after both tragedies. (Both photographs by Hardy Meredith.)

"Mister John" Lightfoot, above, retired in 1984 after having served 24 years in office as sheriff of Nacogdoches County. Soon afterward, county commissioners named their new law enforcement center in his honor. Joe Evans, formerly an officer with the Department of Public Safety, succeeded "Mister John." Below, officials retrieve the remains of Janet Vavra, an employee of Southwestern Bell Telephone Company who was murdered in Nacogdoches. Her remains were discovered on Goat Hill Road in Polk County, and the case remains unsolved. (Both photographs by Hardy Meredith.)

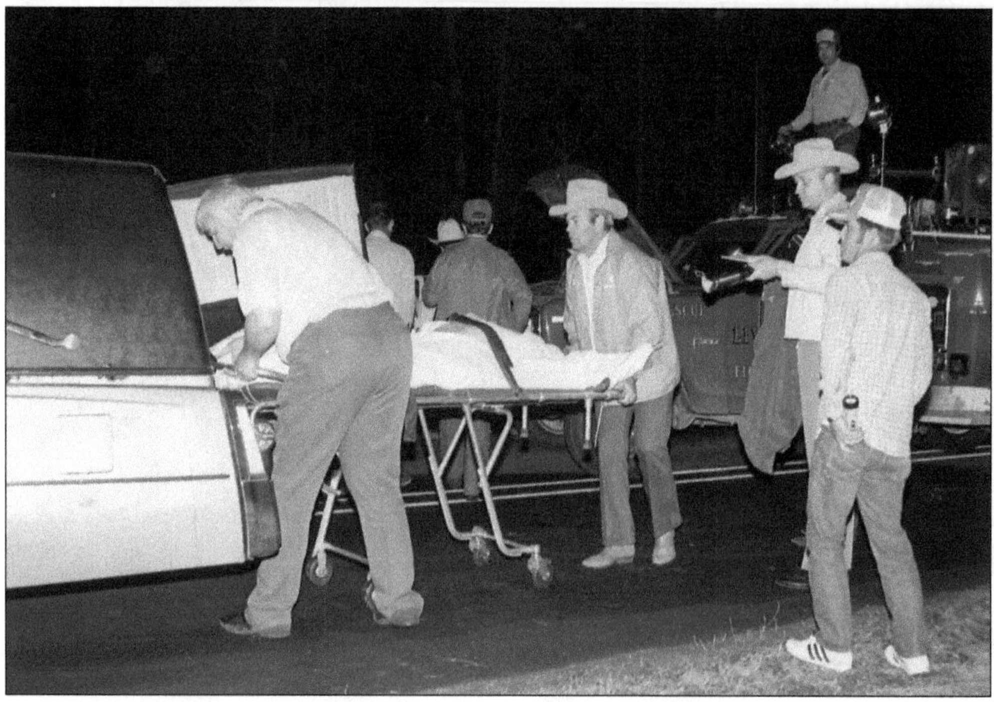

Unidentified Stephen F. Austin State University students view an original copy of the Magna Carta, one of the foundational documents of English and American constitutional concepts dating from 1215, on display in the university's student center. The exhibit was arranged by Drs. Deanne Malpass and Jere Jackson, professors in the university's Department of History. Dr. Malpass was also instrumental in arranging a visit to the university campus for former president Jimmy Carter, shown below being welcomed by Mayor Judy McDonald. When a student asked Carter what he would have done differently in his administration, Carter said, "Send one more helicopter to Desert One," referring to a failed attempt to rescue U.S. embassy personnel held by militants in Tehran, Iran. (Both photographs by Hardy Meredith.)

The Honorable Jack Pierce served as judge of the 145th District Court in Nacogdoches for more than 30 years. Pierce, a Nacogdoches native and graduate of the Baylor School of Law, was the senior judge in Texas at the time of his retirement. Above, Pierce administers the oath of office as "governor for a day" to state senator and lifelong friend Roy Blake while Mae Deanne Blake looks on. Blake was then serving as president pro tempore of the Texas Senate, and it is a tradition that the Texas governor and lieutenant governor leave the state for a day so the president pro tempore may serve as governor for a day. At left, Judge Pierce consults a book of law with Nacogdoches County judge Carl Burrows. (Both photographs by Hardy Meredith.)

Nacogdoches High School athletic director and head football coach Steve McCarty served as chairman of the annual March of Dimes Walkathon fund-raiser for many years. At right, McCarty holds a route marker for the walkathon with Ella Mae Sheffield, 78, who was recognized as the oldest participant in the event. Below is Bob French, who succeeded McCarty at Nacogdoches High School when McCarty became assistant athletic director at Stephen F. Austin State University. French is standing in Dragon Stadium, located on the new high school campus on Loop 224 and Appleby Sand Road. The stands are recycled, having been used formerly at Memorial Stadium on the university campus. (Both photographs by Hardy Meredith.)

Visits to Nacogdoches by George Walker Bush always drew greeters and photographers, even before his election as governor of Texas in 1992. Above, Bush, who, was still managing partner of the Texas Rangers, came to Nacogdoches in January 1988, campaigning for his father, Vice Pres. George H. W. Bush, a candidate for president of the United States. With Bush, from left to right, are unidentified, Nacogdoches attorney Ed Benchoff, Mayor Judy McDonald, Bush, and county Republican Party chairman Steve Lilly. At left, Gov. George Bush is greeted by Pat Mast. (Both photographs by Hardy Meredith.)

Nacogdoches attracted a series of significant visitors in the 1980s. Above, Sam Walton, founder of the Wal-Mart chain of superstores, headquartered in Bentonville, Arkansas, and on its way to becoming the largest retailer in the world, dropped by his store located on North Street in Nacogdoches to check on its progress. Behind Walton is Chamber of Commerce golden greeter Sara Pennington. Below, Stephen F. Austin State University regent Walter Todd, Congressman Charles Wilson, Regent Homer Bryce, and an unidentified associate visit on the university campus. (Photograph by Hardy Meredith.)

Still more visitors stopped by Nacogdoches in the decade of the 1980s. Above, Gov. Bill Clements and Mrs. Rita Clements speak to supporters gathered in the district courtroom of the Nacogdoches County Courthouse. The Clements' were frequent visitors to Nacogdoches, before, during, and after his terms as governor of Texas. Below, a wagon train moved into town in January 1986 to commemorate the Sesquicentennial (150 years) of the Texas Revolution. Mrs. David Campbell chaired the Nacogdoches Sesquicentennial Committee. (Both photographs by Hardy Meredith.)

The Stephen F. Austin State University basketball team enjoyed great success under coach Harry Miller. Above are, from left to right, (seated) Nacogdoches Mayor Pro Tempore Bob Dunn and Mayor A. L. Mangham Jr.; (standing) Stephen F. Austin State University vice president for student affairs Baker Pattillo, Pres. William R. Johnson, and coach Harry Miller. At right, Lumberjack Clarence King perches on the basket following the Lumberjacks' victory over James Madison University in a playoff game. The extended finger of the fan on the right claims that the Lumberjacks are "No. 1," while the extended thumb and two fingers on the hand on the left is the sign of "Ax 'em Jacks!" (Both photographs by Hardy Meredith.)

C. L. Simon was the first African American elected to the Nacogdoches City Commission following the division of the city into wards. Simon represented the Southeast Ward. He was also assistant superintendent of Nacogdoches Independent School District, and before the racial integration of public schools, he had been principal of E. J. Campbell High School. Simon was a devoted horseman who often appeared with an African American equestrian unit in parades in Nacogdoches. The recreation building operated by the City of Nacogdoches on North Street is named in his honor. (Photograph by Hardy Meredith.)

Winter and summer seasons do not often offer such contrasts in Nacogdoches as those suggested by these photographs. Above, a rare snowfall in Nacogdoches blankets Washington Square and creates a Christmas-card atmosphere for the Old Nacogdoches University Building, located on the campus of Thomas J. Rusk Middle School. Below, a summer gathering by a group known as the Rainbow Coalition camped near Nacogdoches for a fortnight of communal living. Residents of the city were sometimes amused and sometimes alarmed by their behavior and the dress—or lack of dress—of some members of the coalition. (Both photographs by Hardy Meredith.)

The Nacogdoches Jaycees included many contemporary and future leaders of Nacogdoches during the 1980s. The Jaycees helped fund the city-owned baseball park and exposition center, operated a haunted house on Halloween, and provided a safe fireworks display for the community's July Fourth celebration. Jaycees, shown left packing a time capsule for Texas's Sesquicentennial, are, from left to right, Brenson Dabney, Leon Hallman, Ben Avery, Miles McCall, Gary White, and Richard King. Below, Jerry Baker, president of Commercial Bank (standing left center), hired a mule team to transport the bank's original safe back home from Branch Patton Hardware Store, where it had been in service since purchased from the bank decades earlier. (Both photographs by Hardy Meredith.)

Being mayor of Nacogdoches is not all fun and games. Visitors to the campus of Stephen F. Austin State University reported a vapor rising from a greenhouse attached to the university's science building, and the city's emergency response program was implemented immediately. Mayor A. L. Mangham Jr. investigated to learn if he should order the evacuation of Memorial Hospital, located only a few blocks away, and he inhaled some of the escaping fumes. Taking no chances, EMS personnel washed the mayor with a fire hose and administered oxygen. Fortunately, the vapor, while fatal to various pests in the greenhouse, was benign as far as the mayor was concerned. (Photograph by Hardy Meredith.)

A. L. Mangham Jr. served in the U.S. Navy from 1940 until early in the 1960s, came home to become president of Fredonia State Bank, served on the city commission for 20 years—13 years as mayor—and received appointment to state commissions from Governors Bill Clements and Ann Richards. Mangham was honored on his retirement with a testimonial roast. Above, Mangham's successor, Judy McDonald, and Gov. Ann Richards applaud "The Mayor." At left, Mangham wipes tears from his eyes from laughing at the humorous comments of Governor Richards. (Both photographs by Hardy Meredith.)

From the 1960s through the 1990s, mayors of Nacogdoches were asked to proclaim every week and month in honor of various charities and activities and photographs of the signing of the proclamation appeared regularly in the *Daily Sentinel*. Above, the Crazy Hats, composed of *Daily Sentinel* staffers, pose with Mayor Judy McDonald in Groucho Marx masks in a familiar setting for regular readers of the newspaper. From left to right are (seated) Kim Barton, Shirley Luna, and McDonald; (standing) J. Lyn Carl, Michelle Ball, Terri Driskill, Hardy Meredith, and Robbie Goodrich. At right, Mayor McDonald bids husband Archie goodbye after the publication of his book titled *Helpful Cooking Hints For HouseHusbands Of Uppity Women*. (Both courtesy of the *Daily Sentinel*.)

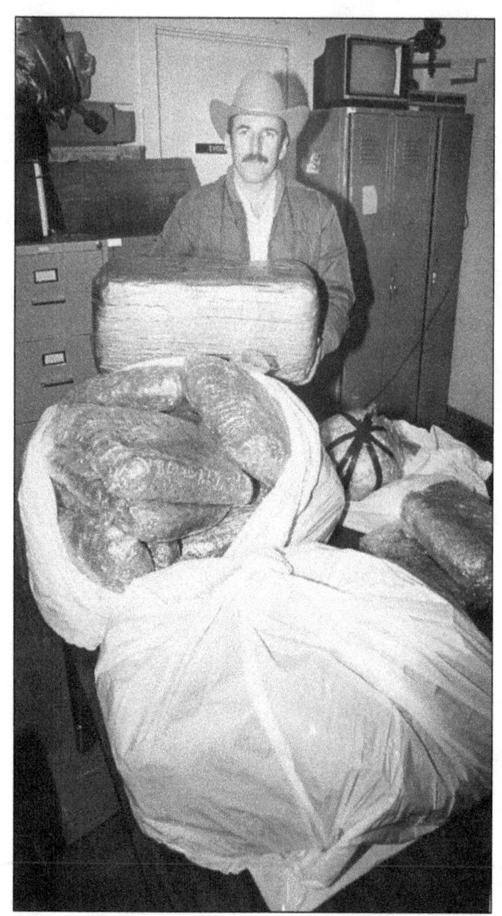

Two products hauled to and through Nacogdoches are featured in these photographs from the 1980s. At left, Deputy Sheriff Craig Mangham shows several bags of marijuana seized from an 18-wheeler skirting Nacogdoches on Loop 224 U.S. Highway 59, a principal highway connecting Mexico with the northeastern portion of the United States. This was also one of the main conduits of this illegal substance to markets in the United States, and Mangham was especially skillful in stopping them. On the other hand, below, Cal-Tex Lumber Company owner Art Patterson and mill manager Barry Ogletree hold up fingers in celebration of the arrival of the first load of logs to their mill, located south of that same Loop 224. (Both photographs by Hardy Meredith.)

Above, Betty Shinn, director of imaging at Nacogdoches Medical Center Hospital and president of the Nacogdoches Chamber of Commerce, and chamber executive director Sidney Abegg examine the chamber's new street map of Nacogdoches. Under Abegg's direction, the chamber oversaw operations at the exposition center and tourism and convention activities and participated with the City of Nacogdoches in industrial and retail economic development. At right, Clarence "Bo" McMichael served as head football coach of the E. J. Campbell Black Dragons football team, assistant coach of the Nacogdoches High School Dragons, and for a time as a member of the board of trustees of NISD. McMichael Middle School, located on Loop 224 South, is named in McMichael's honor. (Both photographs by Hardy Meredith.)

Nacogdoches opened a new post office on University Drive in June 1988, the first time the city's numerous postal headquarters had been located more than a block from the town square. Postal officials explained that the move kept the facility in the center of its service area, because Nacogdoches predominately expanded northeastward. An unidentified postal official observes Postmaster Ken Sims cutting the ribbon to open the post office for its first customers, Congressman Charles Wilson and Mayor Judy McDonald. Below, *Daily Sentinel* news editor J. Lyn Carl presents a framed photograph and news story announcing the retirement of longtime county clerk Hope Skipper to Mrs. Skipper at her retirement reception. Skipper's successor, Carole Roberts, is seated behind Carl. (Both photographs by Hardy Meredith.)

Three Amigos: retired businessman Ed Cole, city manager Jarvis Ammons, and Entex Gas Company manager Bill Presswood share a laugh outside the city commission chambers, located in the Gladys Hampton Building. The red brick streets that surround the city square are behind them, and the former post office—then the city library—can be seen over Presswood's shoulder. Below are city librarian Leigh Cage and Nacogdoches writer Joe Lansdale holding some of Lansdale's earliest publications. Lansdale, who has won an international audience for his fiction in detective stories and other genres, continues to live and write in Nacogdoches in the 21st century. (Both photographs by Hardy Meredith.)

Businessmen Jack McKinney, J. Elbert Reese, and Doug Swearingen, and chamber director Ben Ritterskamp led a community effort that resulted in the construction of Hotel Fredonia in 1955. The hotel operated until early in the 1980s and was reopened, again with community investments, on September 4, 1988. At left, Jack McKinney again raises a replica of the flag of the Fredonia Republic outside his "small hotel," while A. T. Mast Jr., leader of investors who reopened the hotel, encourages well wishers to join them. Below and across the street, workmen with the painting company of Tim Badders add a fresh white coat of paint to the steeple of the First United Methodist Church, located on Hospital Street between North and North Pecan Streets. (Both photographs by Hardy Meredith.)

Nacogdoches's citizens, like people everywhere, come together to make their community a better place. Above, Roy Dean of KJCS Radio greets Doyle Pittman, center, and his son Johnny Pittman, left, who drove by the station's (Make A Smile Happen) M.A.S.H. tent to make a contribution to the city's annual Empty Stocking Fund, which provides Christmas gifts for children who otherwise would not receive them. Below, Nacogdoches residents Charlie Jones and Carrie Butler play a scene in a production of *It Ain't Over 'til the Alligator Sings* by the Lamp-Lite Theatre, located on Old Tyler Road and directed by Sarah McMullan. (Both photographs by Hardy Meredith.)

Above, Weaver, president of the Nacogdoches chapter of the National Association for the Advancement of Colored People, stands in his office on Butt Street, which was renamed in honor of the Reverend Martin Luther King Jr., surrounded by symbols of the civil rights movement. At left, Weaver's daughter, Charlotte Stokes, is surrounded by children enrolled in the Head Start program located on Old Tyler Road, which she directed. The site for the Head Start program was obtained through the assistance of Mrs. Willie Lee Campbell Glass of Tyler, the daughter of Mr. and Mrs. E. J. Campbell. (Above photograph courtesy of East Texas Research Center; below photograph by Hardy Meredith.)

Mike Bay, at right, started working at Mize Department Store in 1963 while still enrolled in Nacogdoches High School as a junior. After graduating from college, Bay taught for three years in Nacogdoches High School and then succeeded Jimmy Simms in the men's department at Mize Department Store. He began acquiring stock in the company and, following the passing of L. D. Pate, was co-owner of the store with Jack Mathews and Pate's daughter, Anita Standridge. Mize Department Store closed on March 17, 2007. Below, Arthur Latin, also known in Nacogdoches as Chef Latin, holds a tray outside his soul food restaurant located on Shawnee Street. Chef Latin's eatery was a favorite even among out-of-town visitors, who came to Nacogdoches just to dine there. (Both photographs by Hardy Meredith.)

Nacogdoches and politics go together. At left, Mayor Judy McDonald and state representative Jerry K. Johnson present an award of achievement to Lera Millard Thomas in one of the historic structures she preserved and restored in Millard's Crossing, a restoration village located on the northern edge of Nacogdoches. Lera Thomas's husband, Albert Thomas, also a native of Nacogdoches, represented the Eighth Congressional District (Houston) for over 30 years, and Mrs. Thomas completed his final term of office following his death. Below, district judge Jack Pierce, right, and Congressman Charles Wilson applaud Gov. Ann Richards, who has just been introduced by state senator Bill Haley for a presentation from the front porch of the Old University Building. (Both photographs by Hardy Meredith.)

An audience gathered on the mall of Stephen F. Austin State University to formally dedicate the statue of Stephen F. Austin, the university's namesake and the Father of Anglo Texas. The statue is located on the west side of the Ralph W. Steen Library, between the Robert McKibben Building, shown at the top, and the R. E. McGee Building, the vantage point for the photograph. Texas governor Mark White dedicated the statue on October 19, 1986. At right is the statue by artist Randy MacDonald of California. The statue was funded entirely by private donations. (Both photographs by Hardy Meredith.)

Nacogdoches Independent School District trustees the Reverend Larry Wade, pastor of Zion Hill First Baptist Church (left); retired coach and teacher Clarence "Bo" McMichael, left center; and banker Bill Sylvester, right, confer with Superintendent Jimmy Partin on district business at a school trustees' meeting. At right, Don Gay, eight-time world champion bull rider, rode in the grand entry of the annual Jaycee Championship Rodeo, held each March at the exposition center. Gay's father, Neal Gay, was the stock contractor for the rodeo, and Don Gay eventually took over that role after he retired from competition. (Both photographs by Hardy Meredith.)

"The thrill of victory. . . and the agony of defeat," are words spoken by announcer Jim McKay at the beginning of each broadcast of ABC's *Wide World of Sports*. This photograph of Nacogdoches High School athlete Gary Russell following his team's loss to R. L. Turner High School of Dallas by a score of 22-11, in a season in which the Dragons won only one game and lost nine, captures the agony well. Russell played for the Stephen F. Austin State University Lumberjacks in 1989 on a team, coached by Lynn Graves, which played for the national NCAA championship in the AA division. (Photograph by Hardy Meredith.)

Nacogdoches landmarks are everywhere in a community billed as "The Oldest Town in Texas," and two of the most prominent are Texas Farm Products, manufacturers of animal feeds and other agriculture and pet products, at left, and Zion Hill First Baptist Church. Texas Farm Products, marketers of Lone Star products, was begun in January 1930 by M. S. Wright and continues into the 21st century under the leadership of Wright's grandson, M. S. "Bud" Wright III. The company's eight-story grain elevator is one of the tallest structures in Nacogdoches. Zion Hill, as the church building is commonly known, was constructed at the beginning of the 20th century as a place of worship for what is now the community's senior congregation of predominantly black worshipers. (Both photographs by Hardy Meredith.)

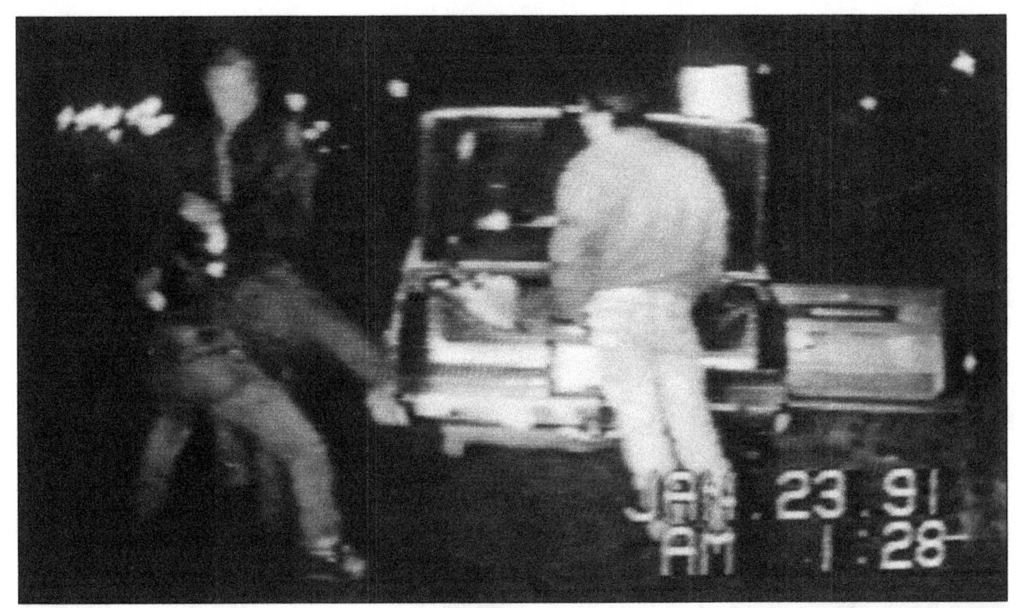

The assault and killing of constable Darrell Lunsford on Highway 59 just north and east of Nacogdoches was captured by a video camera mounted on the dashboard of Constable Lunsford's car in the first such recorded instance in the nation. Lunsford stopped a car containing a driver and two passengers for investigation at approximately 1:25 a.m. on January 23, 1991. The subjects attacked and killed Lunsford, and this frame from the video shows the assault in progress at 1:28 a.m. Law enforcement officers from throughout the state and region attended Constable Lunsford's funeral two days later to support Mrs. Shirley Lunsford, Dianna Lunsford, and Darrell Lunsford Jr. (Both photographs by Hardy Meredith.)

Petite Paige Pattillo of Nacogdoches knew that she wanted to become a twirler before she began her education and was able to fulfill her dream. Constant practice enabled Paige to become the featured twirler for her Nacogdoches High School Dragon Band, the Stephen F. Austin State University Lumberjack Band, and while attending law school in Austin, Texas, for two years, for the University of Texas Longhorn Band, for a total of 10 years. Following graduation from law school, Paige returned to Nacogdoches, where she works in the office of the county attorney for Nacogdoches County. (Photograph by Hardy Meredith.)

The stories of Stephen F. Austin State University and Nacogdoches, Texas, have intertwined since the founding of "the college" in 1923, and these couples are an important part of both. Peggy Wright, at right, is a graduate of the university and served three terms on its board of regents, including a term as chairwoman of the board. Tom Wright is chairman of the board of directors of Texas Farm Products, one of the city's oldest and most significant industries. Behind them is the Tom and Peggy Wright Music Building on the university campus, dedicated on February 21, 1999. Below are Mr. and Mrs. A. T. Mast Jr. at the dedication of the Mast Arboretum on November 12, 1998. (Both photographs by Hardy Meredith.)

Homer Bryce, president of Henderson Clay Products, served on the board of regents of Stephen F. Austin State University longer than any other member. The university's Homer Bryce Stadium is named in his honor. Bryce received an honorary doctorate from the university during commencement ceremonies on December 18, 1993. Shown with Bryce are university president Dan Angel and Regent Sissy Austin. Below, Pres. George H. W. Bush, who spoke at a convocation commemoration of the university's 75th anniversary, chats with Arthur Temple, chairman of the Temple-Inland Corporation, for whom the university college of forestry is named. Dr. Baker Pattillo, center, looks on. (Both photographs by Hardy Meredith.)

George Herbert Walker Bush, the 41st president of the United States, delivered the principal address at an academic convocation in celebration of the 75th anniversary of the founding of Stephen F. Austin State University on April 13, 1999. President Bush addressed the convocation in the William R. Johnson Coliseum and also spoke to a smaller group at a luncheon held in the university center. President Bush lived in Houston following his retirement from public life. (Photograph by Hardy Meredith.)

From left to right, (standing) Dave Watson, Rayford Allen, Bruce Kennon, Doug Clark, and Cliff Whitley; (kneeling) Allen Uhyrek and Sam Allen, members of the WT Gang and modern "bank robbers" from Nacogdoches, pause on North Fredonia Street outside Stone Fort Bank. The WT Gang performed in mock bank robberies and in rodeo parades, some cast as "good guys" and some as "bad guys." Below, Dave Wallace, president of the Nacogdoches Rotary Club, presents a plaque to Harry Garrett, a longtime waiter at Hotel Fredonia, for his good service to club members at their weekly luncheon. (Both photographs by Hardy Meredith.)

When *Daily Sentinel* photographer Hardy Meredith approached a traffic snarl on Starr Avenue near Pecan Park, Nacogdoches police officer Butch Denson approached him and said, "Take my picture!" Denson had been with the department for 15 years and knew Meredith's work well. Below, Mr. and Miss SFA for 2004, Casie Ellison Schmidt and Hardy C. Meredith, the photographer's son, give the "Ax 'em Jacks" sign in front of the statue of Stephen F. Austin, located on the mall of the university. (Both photographs by Hardy Meredith.)

Norman Johnson, a native of Gilmer, Texas, led a roving life as a country music entertainer, Elvis Presley impersonator, radio disc jockey, and talk-show host until he found a permanent home in Nacogdoches. The photograph above was taken at the moment at the annual banquet of the chamber of commerce on October 1, 2001, when Johnson learned he had been named Citizen of the Year for his contributions to the community, especially through Make A Wish Foundation. With Johnson is his wife, Lil. (Courtesy of Norman Johnson.)

Steve Hartz, proprietor of the Old Time String Shop and Mercantile Store, sells and repairs string instruments in his shop on the southeast corner of Plaza Principal. Major figures in the field of musical entertainment visit to utilize Hartz's skills and mingle with local musicians who gather on the String Shop's front porch on Saturday afternoon for informal sessions of old-time traditional music. (Photograph by Hardy Meredith.)

Roy Blake (right), a Nacogdoches businessman, ran an independent insurance agency and served on the city commission and in the Texas House of Representatives and the Texas Senate. Roy Blake Jr. (left) succeeded his father at the insurance agency and served as mayor of Nacogdoches and in the state house of representatives. They are descendants of Bennett Blake, who came to Nacogdoches in the mid-19th century and served as a judge. (Photograph by Hardy Meredith.)

Nacogdoches Medical Center, located at 4920 Northeast Stallings Drive, was founded by a number of medical providers, among them Drs. Ed Klein, Bill Jones, Dennis Coffman, Philip LaBarbera, Burton Crain, Loma Laird, and Ed Furniss. Later the Tenet Corporation acquired and managed the facility. The photograph above shows the main entrance and porte cochere entrance to the women's wing. Below, the emergency entrance is on the left. (Both courtesy of Nacogdoches Medical Center.)

Like most cities, Nacogdoches suffered many significant tragedies since Antonio Gil Y'Barbo founded the community in 1779, particularly from fires such as one that heavily damaged Morgan Oil Company on November 3, 2004. Foam used by the Nacogdoches Fire Department to control the blaze has the appearance of snow, although the fireman said that the fire would have melted all the snow in the area immediately. (Photograph by Hardy Meredith.)

Nacogdoches, despite its growing significance as a regional center, retained a volunteer fire department until well into the 20th century, although the department did have a salaried fire chief after 1930. The first fire chief was E. C. "Bud" Feazell, whose framed picture rests on the bumper of "Old Bertha," now an artifact in the department's museum located on South Fredonia Street behind the Central Fire Station. At left is Capt. Ed Ivy, a 33-year veteran of the Nacogdoches Fire Department, who died while on duty training other firefighters. Ivy came from a family of firefighters: brother Danny and cousins Ricky Ivy and Steven and Richard Arreguin all served in the fire department. (Both photographs by Hardy Meredith.)

Stephen F. Austin State University brings thousands of young people to Nacogdoches who enjoyed the nightlife of various clubs, including Jitterbugs until it was destroyed by fire on April 30, 2006. Viewers watch as members of the Nacogdoches Fire Department continue to battle the blaze. (Photograph by Hardy Meredith.)

On a cold Saturday morning in February 2003, space shuttle *Columbia* attempted to reenter earth's atmosphere at the completion of a successful mission in space. But *Columbia* had sustained damage to some of its heat shields from insulation dislodged during launch, over heated, and began to disintegrate. The debris extended to western Texas, but the preponderance of the doomed craft descended upon Nacogdoches, San Augustine, and Sabine Counties—especially in the city of Nacogdoches—and in a few parishes in western Louisiana. Above is part of the pack of remote television trucks and citizens with attention fixed on one of the larger pieces of debris, which fell in a parking lot located a block from Plaza Principal. Below is a magnified view of the same debris. (Both photographs by Hardy Meredith.)

The *Columbia* tragedy focused the attention of the world on Nacogdoches, as had been the case at Buckingham Palace after the death of Lady Diana and in New York in the wake of the September 11th terrorist attacks. An impromptu memorial sprouted near the piece of the *Columbia* seen on the previous page. Collection of debris continued in Nacogdoches for months with an estimated 5,000 federal workers coming and going for such duty and mostly living in a tent city located just west of town on Loop 224. (Photograph by Hardy Meredith.)

James G. Partin, a graduate of Nacogdoches High School, came back to Nacogdoches as a social studies teacher and then became a school principal and finally superintendent of the school district from 1989 to 1998, when he joined the faculty of another alma mater, Stephen F. Austin State University, in the Department of Secondary Education and Educational Leadership. The smiling scholar to Partin's right is Chris Cagle, son of Dr. and Mrs. Eugene Cagle. At left, Dr. Allen Reed is shown in the sanctuary of Nacogdoches's First Baptist Church, which celebrated its 125th anniversary in 2009. The Reverend Reed became pastor of First Baptist Church on March 1, 1981. (Both photographs by Hardy Meredith.)

Congressman Charles Wilson, who represented portions of East Texas in the state house of representatives and senate and the 2nd Congressional District of Texas for 24 years, donated his papers to the East Texas Research Center in the Ralph W. Steen Library, Stephen F. Austin State University. Wilson came to the research center to open the collection to the public on September 23, 2004. Below, Stephen F. Austin State University president Baker Pattillo, left, and Joe Max Green, chairman of the university's board of regents, right, honor Ed and Gwen Cole at the dedication of the university's art center that was named for them. (Both photographs by Hardy Meredith.)

The Reverend Kyle Childress has served as pastor of Austin Heights Baptist Church for 20 years. He pastors one of the smallest congregations in Nacogdoches but also one with a remarkable record of social ministry. The community's sheltered workshop for Down's syndrome patients began there as the Love Sunday School class, as did the East Texas Aids Project—later known as Health Horizons—the Nacogdoches chapter of Habitat For Humanity, and the area support group for caregivers of Alzheimer's disease victims. (Photograph by Hardy Meredith.)

Above, Austin Heights Baptist Church pastor the Reverend Kyle Childress (right) Zion Hill First Baptist Church pastor the Reverend Larry Wade (center), and the Reverend Lucian Tatum (left), prepare for the Lord's Supper, or communion, in a joint worship service of the two congregations. The churches have been meeting together, with Zion Hill visiting Austin Heights at Christmas and Austin Heights visiting Zion Hill at Easter, since 1970, when the joint services were initiated by the Reverend T. W. Berry of Zion Hill and the Reverend Jerry Self of Austin Heights. Below is the courtyard of the Nacogdoches County Courthouse as it appeared after an extensive remodeling during the first decade of the 21st century. (Both photographs by Hardy Meredith.)

Lucy Dewitt, center, donated property located just north of Nacogdoches on Highways 59 and 259, previously occupied as the headquarters of Kentucky Fried Chicken franchises in East Texas, to Stephen F. Austin State University for the purpose of building a greatly expanded school of nursing. Ground-breaking ceremonies for the new building were held in the spring of 2008. Surrounding Mrs. Dewitt are, from left to right, (first row) Genna Glenz, Carley Meredith, Kelley Mooman, and Allison Tidmore; (second row) Laura Handy, Sarah Donald, James Collins, Lindsey Hickle, Chase Mou, and Matthew Burton. (Photograph by Hardy Meredith.)

The Nacogdoches High School Marching Band received an invitation to march in the annual Rose Bowl Parade on January 1, 2008, and spent most of 2007 raising funds so everyone in the band who wanted to participate could do so. Above, the Dragon band marches past a section in the viewing stands occupied by citizens of Nacogdoches who accompanied the band to California. Below, band director Glen Wells conducts the Nacogdoches Stage Band outside Milam Lodge No. 2, AF&AM, during a banquet lodge members held to raise funds to assist the band. (Above photograph by Hardy Meredith; below photograph courtesy of Dwayne Prestwood.)

Dr. Baker Pattillo, left, eighth president of Stephen F. Austin State University, assumed his duties in 2007. Dr. Pattillo, from Arp, Texas, and a graduate of the university and of Texas A&M University, previously served as vice president for university affairs. Below, Dr. Richard Berry, provost and vice president for academic affairs, is from Longview, Texas, and served as dean of the College of Fine Arts and associate vice president for academic affairs. (Both photographs by Hardy Meredith.)

Until early in the 21st century, Nacogdoches had one state district court, the 145th Judicial District Court, with the Honorable Jack Pierce serving as judge for more than three decades. In 2000, Pierce did not seek reelection, and the Honorable Campbell Cox II, left, won the post. In recognition of the growing number of issues before the court, the Texas Legislature created a second district, the 420th Judicial District Court, and the Honorable Ed Klein, a former district attorney, became judge of this court. Judge Cox's large courtroom was divided during extensive remodeling of the courthouse so each judge would have his own chambers. (Photograph by Hardy Meredith.)

The Nacogdoches Booster Club began in 1921 as the Young Men's Business Club to promote the development of Nacogdoches. Members focused on convincing a legislative site selection committee to select Nacogdoches as host city for Stephen F. Austin State Teachers College. When this effort proved successful, they changed the club's name to the Nacogdoches Booster Club. It is the city's oldest men's organization. Those present for this photograph, taken in April 2008, include, from left to right, (first row) Jefferson Davis, Bryan Holt Davis, Johnny Johnson, Harold Bogan, A. L. Mangham, Farrar Bentley, Jimmy Mize, and Craig Stripling; (second row) Archie P. McDonald, James Raney, Travis Mast, Rick Hurst, Floyd Dobbs, Mike McLean, Roy Blake Jr., and Gary Lee Ashcraft; (third row) Mike Haas, Eddie Overhultz, Rob Atherton, Thad Floyd, Jimmy Partin, Steve Crow, Bill Elliott, and Stan Sisco; (fourth row) Charles Martin, John Young, Travis Clardy, Ed Cole, Tim Hayward, John Ruckel, George Fitch, Campbell Cox, and N. Campbell Cox. Members not pictured are Roger Van Horn, Baker Pattillo, Arthur Speck, Joe Max Green, Dave Wallace, Ron Collins, Roby Somerford, Chris Hancock, Robert Carroll, Lee Britain, Jim Kingham, Jim Jeffers, Bill Gandy, Gary Stokes, Rodney Hutto, and Ed Pool. (Photograph by Hardy Meredith.)

Thomas Kerss, shown left, became sheriff of Nacogdoches County on January 1, 2001, after serving as chief deputy during the administration of his predecessor, Joe Evans, for nearly eight years. Kerss was seen on national television when the media focused on Nacogdoches after the *Columbia* disaster in 2003, when John Lightfoot Law Enforcement Center, where Kerss's office is located, became the crisis management center. Kerss is president of the Texas Sheriffs Association. Below is Chief Jim Sevey, who has served as chief of the Nacogdoches Police Department since December 2005. Chief Sevey is shown in front of the renovated headquarters of the Nacogdoches Police Department. (Both photographs by Hardy Meredith.)

Nacogdoches's oldest living former mayor, A. L. Mangham Jr., right, strolls along Pillar Street toward city hall with the city's incumbent mayor, Dr. Roger Van Horn, left. Mayor Mangham served more than 20 years on the Nacogdoches City Commission, the last 13 as mayor. Mayor Van Horn was reelected to a second term in May 2009. (Photographs by Hardy Meredith.)

Dr. Francis E. Abernethy, left, and Texas Ranger Tom Davis, below, are two tough Texans. Abernethy, a retired professor of English and keeper of the community's historical conscience and compass, is shown in his office on the campus of Stephen F. Austin State University. Abernethy is also the builder of the F. E. Abernethy–La Nana Creek Trail, which parallels the west bank of the creek from downtown Nacogdoches past the university campus to east of Austin Street. Davis has been stationed in Nacogdoches as the Texas Ranger for the area for a decade. (Both photographs by Hardy Meredith.)

The Reverend Monsignor James E. Young, VF, a native of Ohio, has served in Nacogdoches since 1978, including three years at the Catholic Student Center on the campus of Stephen F. Austin State University and 24 years at Sacred Heart Roman Catholic Church. He also has served churches in the Moral and Chireno communities. Below, farmer George "Sonny" Millard brought his onions, carrots, and radishes, among other produce, to town to sell at the farmer's market, and Angela Key was on hand to take some of the fresh vegetables home to cook. (Both photographs by Hardy Meredith.)

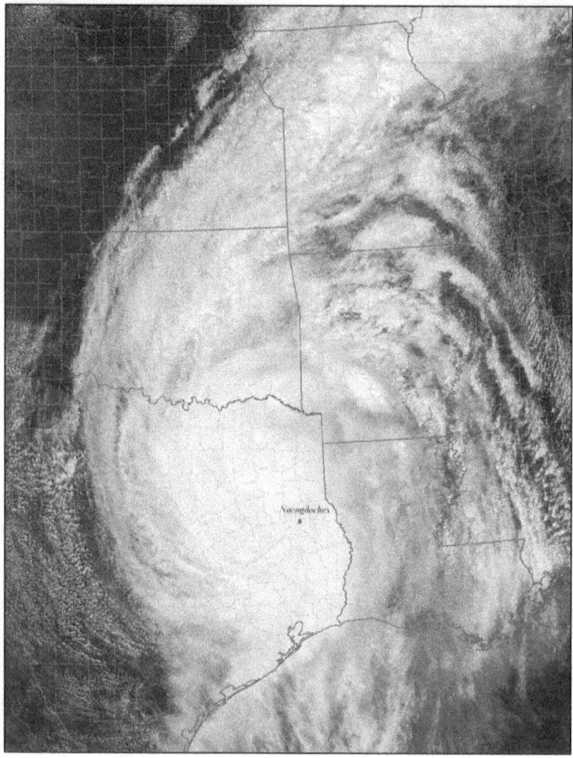

Two killer hurricanes struck Nacogdoches in recent years: Hurricane Rita in 2005 and Hurricane Ike in 2008. The area had received heavy rains and increased wind from hurricanes that struck the upper Texas coast previously, but none were still considered hurricanes, with winds in excess of 75 miles per hour, when they reached Nacogdoches. Rita and Ike had never heard of that rule and just kept coming. Above is damage caused to trees and power lines on Hospital Street by Hurricane Rita, and left is an overview of Hurricane Ike with Nacogdoches designated near the center of the storm. (Photographs courtesy P. R. Blackwell and the Columbia Regional Geospatial Service Center, MODIS data acquired and processed at the Space Science and Engineering Center [SSEC], at the University of Wisconsin-Madison. Additional processing by the Columbia Center.)

Antonio Gil Y'Barbo is represented above by a bronze statue located on the east side of Plaza Principal as a project of Historic Nacogdoches, Inc. Y'Barbo founded the city of Nacogdoches in 1779 near the site of a Spanish mission established in 1716 and abandoned in 1773. This modern Moses led displaced Spaniards across 300 miles of Texas wilderness to a new beginning in East Texas. Below, former mayor A. L. Mangham Jr. strolls along the tarmac of the airport named in his honor and located on the southwest side of Nacogdoches as the sun sets in the west on another day in "The Oldest Town In Texas." (Both photographs by Hardy Meredith.)